THIS CANDLEWICK BOOK BELONGS TO:

_____

_____

_____

_____

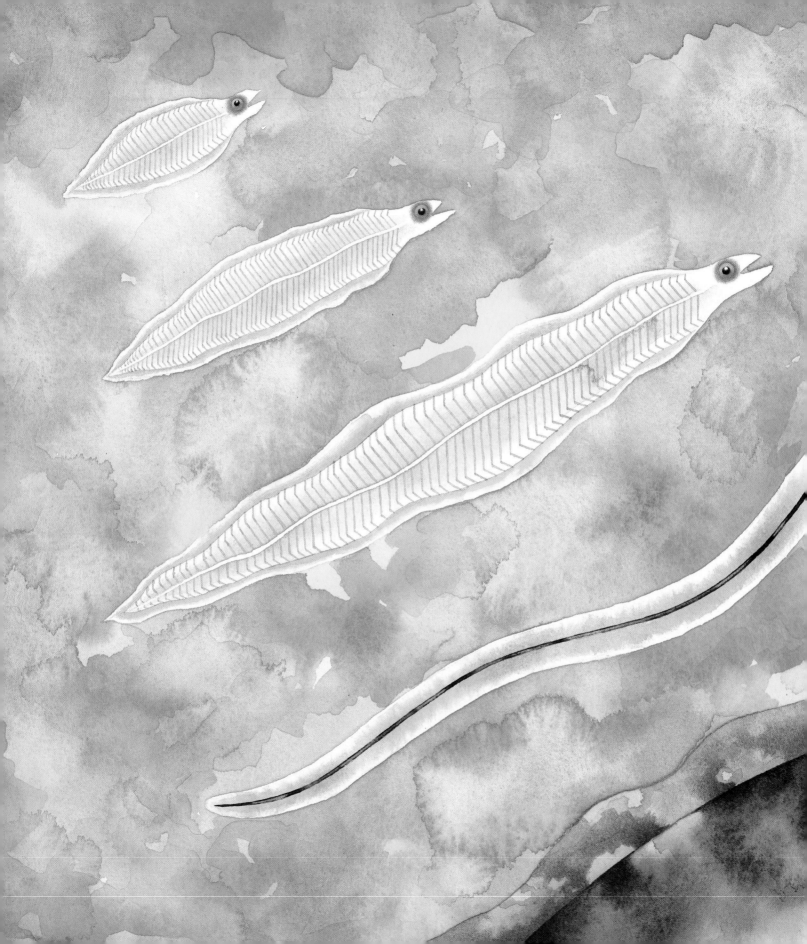

For Martin Llewellyn
K. W.

For my Dad
M. B.

Allen County Public Library

Text copyright © 1993 by Karen Wallace
Illustrations copyright © 1993 by Mike Bostock

Second U.S. paperback edition 2001

Library of Congress Cataloging-in-Publication Data

Wallace, Karen.
Think of an eel / written by Karen Wallace ;
illustrated by Mike Bostock.—1st U.S. ed.
(Read and wonder)
Summary: Text and illustrations discuss the
characteristics and life cycle of the eel.
ISBN 1-56402-180-7 (hardcover)
ISBN 1-56402-465-2 (paperback 1st ed.)
1. Eels—Juvenile literature. [1. Eels.]
I. Bostock, Mike, ill. II. Title. III. Series.
QL637.9.A5W35   1993
597'.51—dc20   92-53131
ISBN 0-7636-1522-6 (paperback 2nd ed.)

10 9 8 7 6 5 4 3 2

Printed in China

The illustrations in this book were
done in watercolor.

Candlewick Press
2067 Massachusetts Avenue
Cambridge, Massachusetts 02140

visit us at www.candlewick.com

THINK of an EEL

Karen Wallace

illustrated by
Mike Bostock

CANDLEWICK PRESS
CAMBRIDGE, MASSACHUSETTS

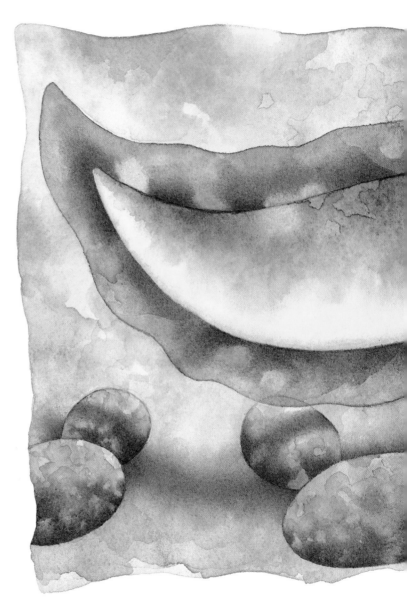

Think of an eel.

He swims like a fish.

He slides like a snake.

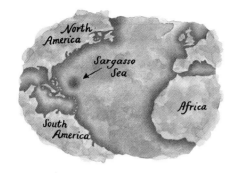

There's a warm, weedy sea
to the south of Bermuda.
It's called the Sargasso.
No wind ever blows there,
no sailing ships sail there.
For thousands of years there
a secret lay hidden:
This salt, soupy sea
is where eels are born.
Deep down where it's blackest,
eel egg becomes eel.
He looks like a willow leaf,
clear as a crystal.

Baby eels are born in early spring.
A real one is only
about this big.

His fierce jutting mouth
has teeth like a saw blade.

He eats like a horse and
swims up through the water.

Young eels from the Sargasso travel either to Europe or to America—whichever

their parents did before them.

Imagine this eel-leaf
and millions just like him
swimming on waves
across the wide sea.
Some are unlucky.
The sea gulls are waiting.
Beaks snap like scissors
through wriggling water.

Eel swims for three years
till he reaches the shore,

but the river's too cold, there's
still snow on the mountains.

Eels arrive in Europe around Christmastime. They wait offshore

So he waits in the water,
turns into an elver.

Now he looks like a shoelace
made out of glass.

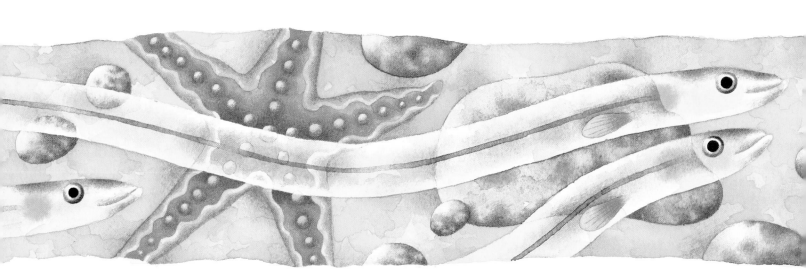

until spring, and as they wait they turn into elvers.

When spring
warms the shoreline,
the smell of fresh water
excites the glass elver.
Into the river
he swims like a mad thing.
He wriggles up rapids,
climbs rocks
around waterfalls.
Riverbanks guide him.
Nothing will stop him.

Eels navigate by instinct.

They always seem to know where they are going.

Around a drowned oak stump,
through twisting green weeds,
a mud hole is hidden.

Mud holes, burrows, and cracks in the riverbed are all homes for eels.

Eel knows without thinking
it's what he's been seeking.
He slips through the ooze.
This hole is his home.

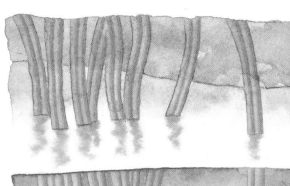

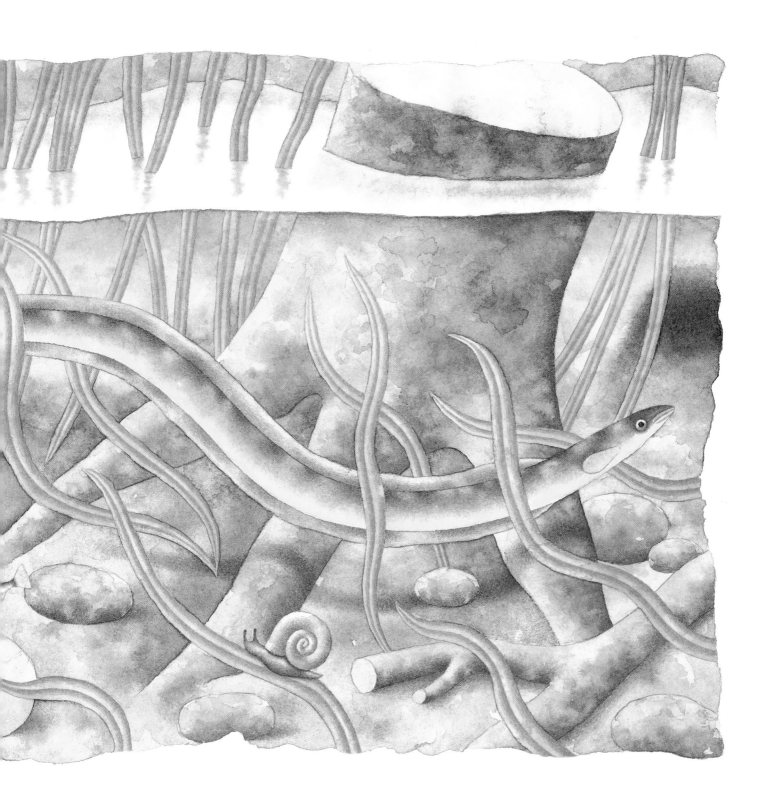

Think of an eel.
After years in the river
he's slit-eyed and slimy
and thick like a snake.
He gulps stickleback eggs,
eats shrimps and small fishes.

shrimp

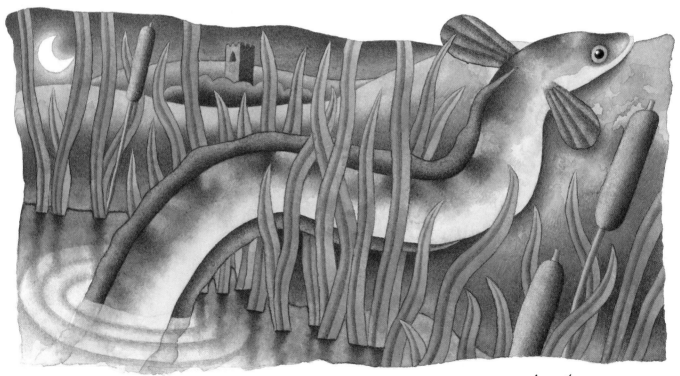

Eels feed mostly at night.

If the river is empty
he swims from the mud hole,
slips through the grass
to steal snails from the pond.

pond snail

An eel can live out of water for two days or longer, if the ground is wet, breathing through its slimy skin.

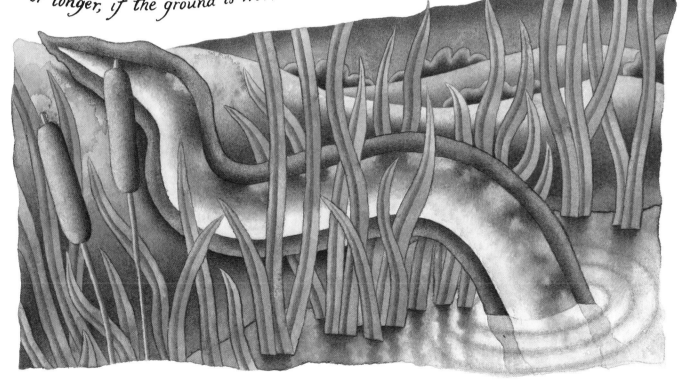

One day eel stops eating.

His stomach is shrinking.

His long winding body

turns silver and black.

Eyes like black currants

bulge into headlights.

Now for the last time

eel slides from the mud hole.

His years in the river

are over forever.

Silver eels usually leave the river in September or October.

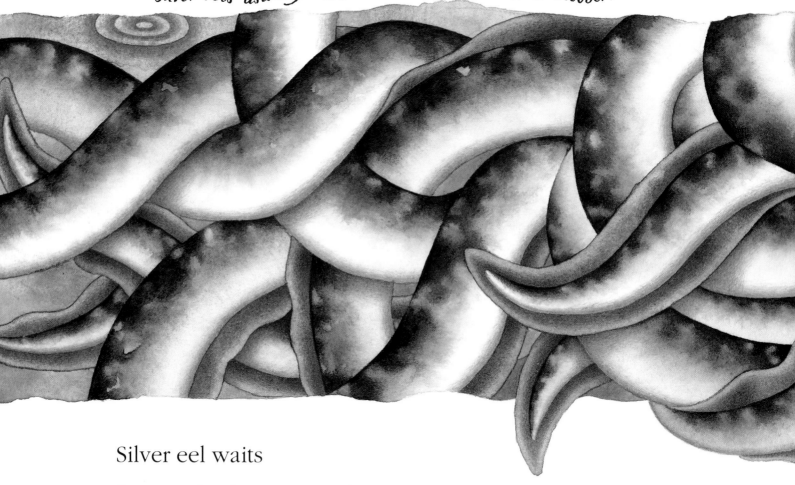

Silver eel waits

for a night that is moonless,

when the rain from the mountains

has flooded the stream.

While they're waiting for a dark night, they sometimes get tangled up in a ball.

Then he slips
down the river, down to
the seashore. The time has arrived
for his long journey home.

For eighty days
silver eel swims through the ocean,
squirms like a secret
from seabird and sailor.

There are millions just like him,

deep down in the water,

swimming silently back

to the Sargasso Sea.

Eels have big eyes for seeing in the dark.

There's eel-tomb and eel-cradle
in the weedy Sargasso.
After eighty days swimming,
not eating, not sleeping,
eel's long, winding body
is worn-out and wasted.
He spills the new life
carried deep in his belly,
then sinks through the sea
like a used silver wrapper.

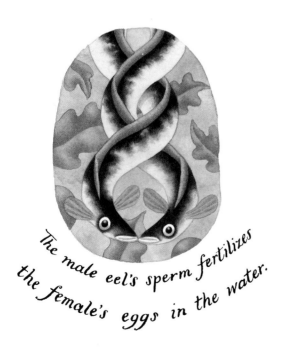

The male eel's sperm fertilizes
the female's eggs in the water.

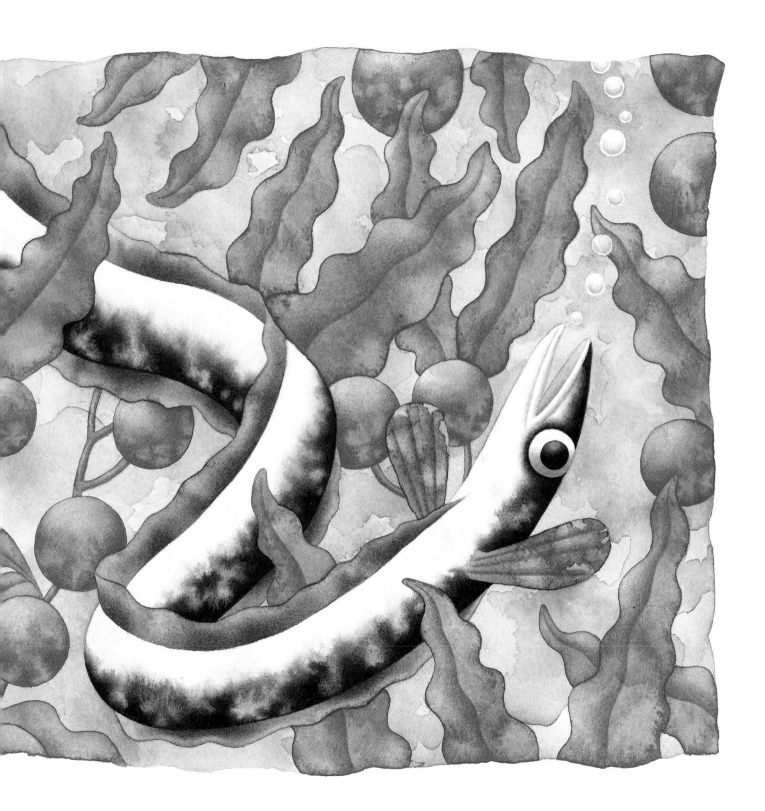

Deep down where it's blackest,
eel egg becomes eel.
He looks like a willow leaf,
clear as a crystal.
His fierce jutting mouth
has teeth like a saw blade.
He eats like a horse and
swims up through the water.

Imagine this eel-leaf
and millions just like him
swimming on waves
across the wide sea...

KAREN WALLACE has spent time fishing in the rivers of Ireland. She says she didn't see eels very often, but "when I did, I couldn't get over how extraordinary they were." Karen Wallace is also the author of *Gentle Giant Octopus,* an NSTA Outstanding Science Trade Book for Children.

MIKE BOSTOCK remembers catching eels as a child. "But reading the text was an education for me. I had no idea they went through so many changes." He enjoys researching the natural history of the animals in his illustrations as much as he does drawing them.